MY WISDOM
THOUGHTS

MY WISDOM THOUGHTS

JAWAD IBRAHIM AL BAHRANI

PARTRIDGE
A Penguin Random House Company

To order additional copies of this book, contact
Toll Free 800 101 2657 (Singapore)
Toll Free 1 800 81 7340 (Malaysia)
orders.singapore@partridgepublishing.com

www.partridgepublishing.com/singapore

A Poem of Introduction

God give me strength and ability to write with justice
So I can write to lead others and never to mislead them
So I can write to teach with a clean language

And my God I ask you, grant me good intentions
So to avoid that which will cause split
That I may write those of faith and history too

So I may write using the sweet language and philosophy
About the people and the tribe whom are alive and dead too
So I can write with good intentions, so I can write with wisdom

So I can write with clean heart and without fear
And never with bad language and never with weakness
But so to write for that reason of good faith and justice

So I can write without hate or favourism
So I can write for a friend but also against a foe
that I should never write of what has not happened but reality

But also I should write of fictions of tales and stories too
That which strike in the mind so others can benefit with
So I can write of the past of what has really happened

Every possible interval I can write of what I can advise
And that will create no problems and may cause hatred
But I can write what others can benefit and bring happiness

So I can write with good aim and with consideration
And allow myself to pass through discipline and fairness
And never with broken language have which leaded to wrong path

So I can write with a brave heart and use my intelligent
To choose my words and not to rush
And use my sense with exactly language

So I can write and understand what my intentions are
Never to be injustice because I choose favourism
Others can blame me that I was not fair to them

So I can write very important, a steady poem
So to increase the sweetness and more they want hear
With the best of the language of wisdom and philosophy

These are my intentions and are my limits
So not cause inner pain to others and think I had intended to
Yet you cannot please all, to please all is to please none.

This is the roughly translation of my Swahili introduction poem.

Jawad Ibrahim Ahmed - 17-9-2014

Acknowledgment

It will be very much unfair if I will not appreciate all the help receiving from others,

Who share their pain taking in either helping me with English Grammar of this book or helping me in typing or even bare with me in bothering with their valued time in middle of night just to listen of what I have written or switching on the light when one enjoying his sleep. So, in this small paragraph I take this opportunity to thank you all who share your good moments with me in enable me to complete this book of MY WISDOM THOUGHTS till it reach on the desk of publisher. My particular thank should go to Saleh Shaibani my nephew, Nasser Rashid Mbwana my wife nephew, and especially my wife Saida Abdulla Ali Shaibany for her patience and bare with me all those years of my writing no matter what time in the night. Also I will not forget my son Naqeeb who also gave many helping hands, one way or the other, either typing, correction or suggestions. Yet lastly my sincere thanks should go to my grandsons Humud Abdulla Al Sumry and Nadheem Al Bahrani, for their contributions in making book covers as computer graphics as I designed it.

Thank you all, you good people.

Jawad Al Bahrani
21st December 2014.

Foreword

Since my childhood reading was one of my keen interest, I would spend most of my school money to buy comics and other Swahili story books, but I would like to spend my time reading something, something amusing, intertaining, or real happening, even some fiction books did draw my attention and will read them. Most of my over spending books I use to buy were of "The cases of Perry Mason" and Ian Flaming "James Bond" etc. From these books I have learned and improved in understanding of the English Language and practice of what I have learned and using those new words, so many of my childhood friends who knows and spoke proper English language, use to laugh at me when I pronounce some words wrongly, but from them is where I have corrected my self in using proper words and proper pronunciation.

Though I had very good school teachers of whom from them I have learned so many knowledges, such as history, religion, science, mathematics, geographic, and of course our own culture and heritage, and that including using phrases of languages examples by coating wise sayings or philosophy thoughtsof those wise people before me as an encouragement to understand a matter of the subject or situation of the purpose of that teachers teaching clearly, but yet I have learned, and from my teachers I am thankful, thankful for yesterday, today and the rest of my life as I am now passing on the knowledge of their education to my children and my grandchildren and to you my dear reader.

My intention of writing this book is, first, I enjoy philosophy, I like to learn and to know more, and I am proud that from the beginning of Adam, a human mind can create words of wisdom or wise saying and philosophy thoughts to be used as knowledge or persuasion to encourage others to do of what is right and avoid of wrong doing.

To me these people who use their mind in creating such wisdom thoughts for us all, have performed wonders in knowledge of this kind of high level just by using few strong words with very deep meanings and very affective, should have very special place in our hearts forever to remain for their creation of this great knowledge which they have left behind for us.

I am not a scholar, neither a highly graduated person, but was educated and self taught person and do respect the value of education and knowledge, and by God I will always remain thankful that education exist for us from those before us who took great pain with their wise minds in insisting that a child should learn so he should grow to teach and live in a civilise world and never literacy or like a wild animal.

Yet many thanks of all the knowledge of knowledges should go to God, who is the only teacher who taught us civilisation and brought us religion through his messengers whom they have teach us with great wisdom of how to live with love and peace and have faith in him in this earth, but also that there is life after death which we should believe that he has created for us another living life which will never end, known as heaven.

My book "MY THOUGHTS OF WISDOM" is not as a solid proof or the only right thoughts of wisdom, but to be considering as an individual thinking, as freedom of expression is for everyone to accept or to deny it, that is your judgement my dearest reader.

It is my hope that what so ever I wrote and my mind has created in this book is not for my own good only but for all the mankind, either to remind others or to teach or maybe I have repeated what others have already said before me, all those million of years since Adam, of which I have no knowledge about, and if so, then our goals and intentions are the same in creating and preserving these knowledge of Thoughts of Wisdom to be used for the better of mankind and never the worst.

Your Author

Jawad Ibrahim Ahmed Al Bahrani
7th June 1999

Preface

In the name of Allah the most precious and most merciful. I take this opportunity to explain my understanding on the words of wisdom. Wisdom is a blessing from God to us all to use it to inspire one another, from angels to human and even and everything in between. In his books which God sent them to us, so to learn and understand his teaching what is right and what is wrong, in other words, what is acceptable and what is not where one needs to be rewarded or be punished. If by any chance, one had a chance to read any of God's holly books which are Taurat, Zaboor, Ingle(Bible) or Furqan (which is Qur'aan) which were sent to us through his messengers David (Daud) Moses (Musa) Jesus (Issa) and Muhammad, God granted his prophets with philosophical language of wisdom to teach us and so to make us understand and believe in God existence and never otherwise in true and strong faith. Most of the words God used were very logical and such a sweet language that one would like to read again and again. Nevertheless, all of his messengers whom served him and obey his commandments were task to pass the same knowledge of his wisdom to their followers by using many phrases from his books so we his creation should be inspired when listening or reading his teaching and narrate to others even a line from these books.

The question here is why me? Who am I to write such a high standard knowledge of language using phrases of wisdom? Am I a student of such kind of people whom are known of their writing and teaching of wisdom? The answer is no, I am just a simple person, but then, from where have I acquired this knowledge of writing and creating words of wisdom? My answer to this question is, I believe that I have inherited this knowledge from my ancestors who according to the books of "MUJAMMA'A ASMA'A AL ARAB" (Dictionary of Arab names) books, were philosophers and writers, the information of the history can be found through Bahrani tribe pages in those books which are in two volumes, you will find that the art of writing is embedded deep into my DNA, the tribe of AL BAHRANI shares their lives to be known as writers, philosophers, doctors etc. Yet I have faith within me that almighty God has gifted me with this power of knowledge as he did to those before me. Among those before me in my tribe are the following names:-

1. Alshardal Al kaabi – Al Bahrani (A doctor before and after coming of Islam. He converts to Islam in the hand of Prophet Muhammad.

2. Kamal-din Haytham bin Ali Al Bahrani. 1280AD (Philosopher and linguist).

3. Yusuf bin Ahmed bin Ibrahim (Who writes many books, among those is a book by a title "PEARLS OF BAHREIN" 1772AD.

I conclude this preface by thanking God for granted me with the knowledge of writing and the mind of wisdom and be able to contribute this gift of knowledge to others through my books among them MY WISDOM THOUGHTS, MY POEMS. I only ask my reader to take of what he/she agrees with it and leave a side of what he/she does not believe in it. After all I am only human with a limited knowledge and not to compete but to follow those before me in sharing what God has given us to do for a better of mankind and never for the worst.

Jawad Al Bahrani
8th October 2014.

Introduction

If there are any thanks to give, then my parents should be my first priority, as from these wonderful people where my originality came from made me feel proud of what and from where I belong and came from. Oman is my country and by the will of God is where where he chose for all our generations to be and was, I may be born not on this land of my ancestors but was born in a small tiny island in East African Coast where the waves of Indian ocean still sings loudly on the beaches of that island known as ZANZIBAR where my parents immigrate from Oman and chose Zanzibar by the God's will as their second home, yet to me and my brother's and sister's is our first home as it was the place we saw when we opened our eyes, grew and earn our education there.

I have worked in various places but most successful was a seaman in the ships between 1953 to 1957. After that I joined the Zanzibar electricity board as engine attendance in the power station from 1961 to 1968.

Since my childhood when still I was in the school, my keen interested was photographing. In 1964 I started my home studio and photographic coverage on occasions and different events to earn my extra pocket money for me and my new family as I was married to such wonderful person from a very highly respected family and I had to persuade my father that for me she is the only girl of my choice and no other can take her place in my heart and still up to this day that I am writing this introduction, she is my only love of my life. From her she has bared from me five wonderful children. Today they have grown up to men and women and they all got married and earn their respects from our society and bared their own children of which then made us to be very proud for having twenty one grandchildren. May God bless them all.

In 1975, I left Zanzibar to look for better prospects and better future for my family and found it here in Oman, my home land. The land of my ancestors, after working in Bahrain, stayed for sometime in England and worked in Ajman, UAE till 1977 of where I joined Ministry of Information in Oman as T.V cameraman and became senior cameraman with privilege of teaching new comers to become future generation cameramen and thank to God that I have achieved that ambition that today most of field Oman Television cameramen are my students and holding all the responsibilities of producing almost all the programs, documentaries as well as news coverage with no single non Omani cameramen holding that position after 20 years of hard service and responsible tasks to fulfil. I have requested to be transferred to film director as well as giving advises to our young cameramen and new comers. From them I have earned their respect that they never call me by my first name but always address me as "BABA JAWAD" or Mr. Father.

I am proud of them and pray for them from the deep of my heart that they too should fulfil their missions and do of what is best for their country.

I would like to thanks all members of my family for their many donation of their valuable time in helping me either typing in the computer or listening to my Thoughts of Wisdom seeking for their advice or knowledge.

1. War, wherever it happened it may end either with victory, defeat or understanding, but also will leave behind forever to remain the most unforgettable and painful memories, and what a high price those nations has to pay. War can heal its wounds but never the scars.

2. Even fools sometime does and act like wise, and wises people do foolish things, but who be willing to support a wise fool rather than a foolish wise

3. We need to build strong and intelligent forces to defend our countries not by its quantity but by its quality.

4. I will bare no more burdens after my death, as life itself is a hell of a burden for one to carry

5. If technology is a knowledge aiming to preserve mankind and not destroying it, than I accept it.

6. When storms rage in the sea, so many lives perish or lost, but for those who intrude in the sea and not for those who are living with it

7. So many people do speak wrongly about others yet very few do the same about themselves.

8. If you believe that corruption can solve or easy your problems, than you must also believe that yours is a corrupted mind.

9. I can bare the whipping pain on my body rather than torments pain in my heart.

10. Why are you trying to make matters too complicated by ignoring the fact when the fact itself has no complication?

11. For the sake of our nation dignity, it is not important of who I am but of what I do for my country.

12. Millions Of people use these words "I LOVE YOU" when they only mean, "I DESIRE YOU".

13. Sometime a strong man heart becomes weak just by a glimpse of a woman.

14. He, who does respect his word of honour, will gain reputation among the respectable people as they will honour and respect him too.

15. You must use your influence practically to convince your children that they must strive to gain their standard of education high.

16. Sometimes changes in life bring better moments of joy and we accept it, and if changes bring hardship and bitter way of life, we regret it.

17. Do not destroy and cut trees down and put the blame on the wind.

18. Even strong and wise people sometime are cowards, no matter how brave they are.

19. When you come to find that your trusted friend supports your enemy, than it is your enemy who should realise what kind of friend he has gain.

20. There are moments in life where loneliness is the best medicine for one to have, yet sometime it tortures deep within mentally.

21. Any achievement won by a person with his good deeds done in any place in the world, should be regarded as an ambassador for his country.

22. He who plant crops will benefit both, food and income. He who plant flowers, did it just to satisfy his heart desire.

23. When you know it is wrong, why then keep on doing it? Does it make you happy or regret it after, do you consider?

24. Learning is to be educated, and education is must for everyone, yet it is part of life great achievement.

25. Glory is a pride of that nation which has conquered the internal war against all and fulfils its people needs. That is a nation which has won even Gods blessing.

26. The thoughts of death always put fear in human minds, yet, so many have the courage to play with death in their games just for the sake achieving their aim.

27. When talking became exhaustion, silence is the best energy for the mind.

28. Never misjudge all the right done of a person for just one wrong mistake.

29. Death is an inevitable end, no matter when or where we will meet with it, crying will never return a soul back to a dead body nor will bring back life again, so please do not cry for my death but pray for my soul to rest in peace.

30. You should accept a friend for what he is and not for what he has.

31. If you ignore to repair the crack today, you will build the whole wall tomorrow.

32. What is mine is mine, what is yours is yours, then why you are insisting in taking mine when I did not take yours?

33. There are times when you need wisdom to deal with circumstances.

34. To preserve our heritage and culture is to safeguard our civilisation.

35. For me, I am willing to be lack of experience rather then lack of wisdom.

36. How painful I felt when I watched my elder brothers fight and exchanging blows on each others face, while they were bleeding with blood I was shedding tears and agony in my heart.

37. Why should I believe those who do not believe of what I believe.

38. Being a human being, why not that I should do something worth for mankind and leave behind a good example for all generation to come and let history tells about of what I have done.

39. Once I ask my children, who is the most dangerous and cruel creature God ever created? These were their replays, one said a "LION", the other said a "SNAKE" and last said a "DEVIL", but poor human being he forgot himself.

40. Even the powerful one's do have fear, they can create a war, and go to fight that war, but their main fear is how that war will end and at what cost.

41. Shedding tears will never mend the broken heart and never will bring back life to the death.

42. Even wise people sometimes are unwise for being too much wise.

43. By hating me, are you really gain self-satisfaction or torments within your heart?

44. I have been created to live, peaceful I want to live, but mankind does not leave me alone to live.

45. One do not judge the deliciousness of food by its colour or decoration but by it's test.

46. Millions Daily speaks, write and praise of many famous people, but very few do the same to ADAM, the father of our mankind.

47. I can bare the lost of my wealth or the condition of my health, but never will I bare to loose my God's faith.

48. You can try to persuade someone to believe of what you do, but never will you force him to believe of what he does not, as force is not the only source of power for any one to change his faith.

49. A BEDOUIN can sell his wife's gold or slaughter his only goat just to give you his hospitality as his guest.

50. Some poor people who became penny less would go rather begging or die with hunger than steal.

51. If you have more than enough, than give to those who do not have anything, God will give you more than you know.

52. He who does not care to cure his illness should not be ignored, otherwise if you will not cure him today you will do for hundreds tomorrow.

53. How much kindness you will do to others, how much helpful you will be to the closed one, but will mankind treat you the same?

54. They are too disciplined and preserving, sometimes too tough just to protect me as I am their jewel on the crown.

55. No matter how much I may give or all the services I may render in my whole life, yet I can not repay of what my parents has given me.

56. A professional artist who performs with an amateur can loose his standard of quality if he allows his students to take the reins.

57. When nations compete in tournaments, it is not the winning that counts most but above all, the friendship, the pride and also gaining of others love of which they will take with them in their hearts back to their countries.

17/01/88   6.25a.m

58. Man should leave behind good example of what he has done.

17/01/88   7.50p.m

59. I believe in curing the disease, no matter how or with what, I respect the Result.

17/01/88   8.20p.m

60. In every story there is a tale; in every happening there is a story to tell.

18/01/88   2.00a.m

61. Persuasion is a best technique for a salesman to have, he should sell to you of what you did not intend to buy.

17/01/88   10.14a.m

62. In some cases, self-satisfaction is necessary for someone to do things his own way.

18/01/88   11.10a.m

63. Do not allow to be betrayed by an attraction of a woman's beauty, as where there is beauty sometime there is evil too.

18/01/88   6.06p.m

64. Any sincere leader of any country should respect without discrimination all his countrymen regardless of their faith, creed or race.

18/01/88   10.45p.m

65. Naturally, a weak fears a strong, but when a weak becomes strong, than it is that strong who should do the worry.

18/01/88   10.55p.m

66. You can cure a broken bone but not a broken heart.

19/01/88   8.00p.m

67. You can throw away a broken glass but you can not throw away a broken arm.

19/01/88   8.12p.m

68. When a dog bark too much in the night and disturb, you curse him, but when you come to find out the good reason for his barking, you praise and even kiss him.

20/01/88   3.17p.m

69. Criticism is a challenge and a key to find out of what we did was wrong or right, it is also one of the solutions to solve our problems as constructive as well as destructive.

20/01/88   8.00p.m

70. Sometimes regret comes too late, for you can try to heal the wounds but you can not wipe the scars.

21/01/88   7.05a.m

71. Guide me to the right path so I can leave my footprints behind for others to follow as well, and may God guide you to your destination.

21/0188   7.25a.m

72. If you have denied fact to be true and accept lies as truth than you have sold justice and bought injustice.

21/01/88   9.02p.m

73. You may request of what you want but you should accept of what you get.

21/01/88   3.17p.m

74. The world today is like a big jungle, to survive you should be a predator and never a prey.

21/01/88   5.09p.m

75. In life, every normal person has a duty to do something of value.

23/01/88   5.45p.m

76. It does not matter how much time or hardship one has to face to perfect an act, what counts most is the success of that act.

23/01/88   4.58p.m

77. Through collective efforts we can achieve our goals, we need to unite together.

24/01/88   5.55a.m

78. Though you may not need his advice, but by listening to him proves that you care and respect his feelings towards you.

24/01/88   6.03a.m

79. I can never say it more beautiful and understandable, better than what others have said before me, sometimes too much adding colour can spoil the paints.

24/01/88   6.17a.m

80. If you like the song, you should also give credit to the composer as well as the writer and not only the singer.

24/01/88   6.35a.m

81. Sometimes I wonder why I feel so strange in this world of where I belong.

24/01/88   6.40a.m

82. A reasonable person will never seek enjoyments at his friend's expense; this habit may cost him more to repay than what he has gain.

24/01/88   7.00a.m

83. We should not build our dreams with thoughts and imaginations but with reality.

24/01/88   5.40p.m

84. If we always judge matters by our thoughts and not reality, then we have done so much injustice to the fact.

24/01/88   5.43p.m

85. Why do we let our selves get involve in a groundless arguments when the fact is there to defend it self.

25/01/88   5.45p.m

86. Many out of many well known people died and are forgotten, but a person who became a legend, though died, he is always remembered.

25\01\88.   11.37.p.m.

87. When you refuse to attend to an invited function of a friend just because he did not attend yours before, than you have committed a worse mistake, as you are now not repaying but avenge him to satisfy your personal feelings.

25\01\88   5.58a.m.

88. If you do not agree with others advice with a matter which concerns you, try to understand that advice with your heart, maybe they can solve the situation.

89. it's not a parent's wealth that will satisfy their children ambition, sometimes a child may have dreams of his own which are beyond any wealth.

25\01\88.   10.05p.m

90. it's very hard to believe that in this generation still time became valueless for other's to realise.

25\01\88.   10:05p.m.

91. When a baby cries with a pain he suffers, it is the mother who suffers most of the pain, spiritually and mentally and shedding tears within her heart for her poor baby's agony.

26\01\88.   4.30p.m.

92. There was a lullaby my mother use to sing for me when I was a child, which says:-

HOWA! HOWA! My dear child. Please, please do not cry, as your cry will make me cry stop your tears and save them till that day that I will die.

26\01\88.   4.40p.m.

93. Wedding gifts given to a newly wedded couple will not only show love and care from friends and relatives, but also it will help them to climb other steps in their new responsible life.

28\01\88.   9.00a.m.

94. Who ever die will never come back immortal but his memory lives forever till eternity.

28\01\88.   12.57p.m.

95. He who walks on a rough road, walks carefully by watching every single step he move on ahead with, he also concentrate and direct his conscious in every step he take to avoid stumbling or getting lost.

27\01\88.   8.29a.m.

96. There comes circumstances in life which can force you to accept of what you are not use to it, even the forbidden fruit you will eat it.

29\01\88.   6.20p.m.

97. By sweating, that does not prove that you have worked so hard and with satisfaction, only the results of your work will prove and speak for you.

31\01\88.   1.52p.m.

98. Sometimes just a tiny fly can be so disturbing than a child.

31\01\88.   2.00p.m.

99. A woman is a long life partner, but depend what kind of a woman one chooses. For me, I would prefer my partner to be kind, wise, tolerant or poor I don't mind, but never to be mean and foolish, or rich but stupid one, that is not my kind of a woman.

21\07\89.   10.27a.m.

100. It needs courage and patience to deal with a foolish friend more than you need with a wise foe.

21\07\89.   10.30a.m.

101. One can gain a friend in a single moment, but once loose him; it may take his lifetime to regain him again.

21\07\89.   11.05a.m.

102. He who does not fulfil his promise is not a gentleman and an uncivilised person never to be trusted.

8\08\89.   7.30p.m.

103. I think it is for the better rather than worst for a child to correct his school mistake by himself rather than to be corrected by his parents.

8\12\89.   7.35p.m.

104. Sometime I wonder what was a reason that has sealed that mouth which was always speaking truth.

Dec\89.

105. A civilised person always deals with circumstances in a civilised way.

31\01\88.   5.35.p.m.

106. One can rebuild a destroyed city in a matter of no much time, but it may take him whole his life time to try to mend a broken heart.

1\02\88.   7.47a.m.

107. If you are always a person who offer a helping hand to others when they are in needs, then do not accept the same from them when you will be in need.

1\02\88.   8.00a.m.

108. A very good leisure time will earn you nothing more than pleasure, but a hard and tiresome work will fill your pockets.

1\02\88.   8.22a.m.

119. No matter what differences occurred between parents and their children, to parents children are their precious gems, but do our children have the same feelings for us?

1\02\88.   5.33p.m.

110. Do not show your hate-rade to those who do not agree in what you believe, as this will not only create heat of hate but may put a foundation of misunderstanding between you and others.

11\02\88.   11.07p.m.

111. Many for some reason or another do have reasons to revenge, but there is no more dangerous and cruel than a woman's revenge.

2\02\88.   6.02a.m

112. There are two things in life that plays major roles in our daily life, fate and luck, each among these do knock on our doors unexpectedly either bring miserable or happiness, as these two guests are just waiting around the corner and no one knows which among the two will knock to whose door.

2\02\88.   5.02.p.m.

113. The force of evil is strong enough to penetrate in our minds, but the force of our will power is much stronger and act as shield and not to allow the evil thought to pass through, if we will not willingly allow it.

3\01\88.   6.00a.m.

114. You can cure a disease with your self-medicine but never to a hunger.

3\01\88.   6.26a.m.

115. Do not judge me by my look or personality just to believe of how good I am, but by my attitudes, manners, behaviour and my heart.

12\02\88.   7.27p.m.

116. There are times where a man's heart becomes an easy target to be fooled just by looking at beautiful things.

4\01\89   11.25a.m.

117. Some mouths exaggerate more than reality, so clever in their words more than the fact, but when fact prevail and truth became clear, then even a hiss sound never to be heard from that same mouth.

20\07\89.   11.23p.m.

118. Woman is man's long life partner, depend of what kind of a woman one would like to have. For me I will prefer a kind, tolerant, wise even though poor rather than a mean, foolish and a stupid rich one.

21\07\89.   10.27a.m.

119. He, who does not fulfil his promise, is not a gentleman and not to be trusted, even with his own life.

11/07/89.   11.59a.m.

120. A wise person will try so hard not to repeat his previous mistake again, only a fool will not bother.

8\12\89 7.30p.m.

121. Even to this day I wonder what is the reason which has made that mouth which use to speak only the truth and now seal itself off and not to be heard again.

8\12\89.   8.00p.m.

123. Always mistakes worsen the situation; we should try to avoid them not to happen again and never to allow mistakes overcome our mind to repeat again and again.

17\12\89.   7.40p.m.

124. He who seek education, will never bother what kind of a classroom he is going to sit in, either an air condition room or under the shade of a tree, but the important issue here is what will he be educated.

21\01\90.   10.32a.m.

125. It is our acceptation that tomorrow will bring better hope than what we had yesterday.

22\01\90   10.30P.M.

126. In this world, there are some people who spend many of their time writing for others to read, but also their are those who like to read and do not care who the writer is.

7\02\90.   12.30a.m.

126. When the sun rise, a new day is born, maybe it may bring good surprises for you me and everyone, so let's be bright and wise, to face this day with fun.

3\03\90   9.14p.m.

127. Evil is bad, but a human being is worse than evil, as no evil is known till man perform it.

9\04\90

128. Force can be used as power, but itself has its limit, either above or below other powers, here is where force faces a problem of who will be master of that force.

9\04\90.   10.27.a.m.

129. If you try to stop a child not to play with a lighter, he will cry and throw himself on the ground crying for it, but if you let him to play with it and burn his finger, he will throw that lighter on the ground and never to touch again.

15\08\90   12.00a.m.

130. Many of us do not like to swallow a bitter medicine and find it hard, yet sometime we face with more bitterness of hard life, yet we could not help it and we swallow.

17\08\90.   10.05p.m.

131. A person who pays a visit to your house should be welcome, but only after you know the purpose of his visit.

17\08\90.   10.15p.m.

132. It is not of poor or richness that make one's life better and happy, but of how to overcome all obstacles and necessities of life, if only you have enjoyed with your life with what you have, than you may regard yourself as a successful person.

17\08\90.   10.40p.m.

133. Photographs are to show you the present, to remind you of the past and to preserve our future as history, for always to remain.

Nov 1989.

134. You may enjoy your laugh today, laugh as much you can laugh, but as your laugh start to end then prepare yourself for the cry, and when you will start to cry, you will cry and cry and nothing can make you stop crying.

17\10\90.   7.12.pm

135. If one finger is not strong enough to hold or lift things, than you need to use all your fingers to gain strength.

9\01\91.   12.12a.m.

136. When birds sing no more, and sky is completely empty, and silent has dominated the outside world, than mankind should wake up to realise that earth has reach its ending days.

9\01\91.   12.12a.m.

137. A gift from a dear friend should be valued by it's presentation as a gift and never price wise.

22\02\91.   11.25a.m.

138. When truth does not wish to prevail and hide behind a curtain, then it should not be disturb or forced to be expose openly, and we will do so, we may find very hard to face or accept it.

9\04\91.   1.52a.m.

139. For the sake of a perfect results always rely on profession.

Aug 1990.

140. It needs wisdom to solve a dangerous situation when a know how hand is far away to reach in time.

31\03\93.   11.23p.m.

141. There are time to do particular things and things to do in particular time.

2\04\93   9.05.p.m.

142. There are things we believe without seeing them and things that we have to see to believe them.

20\09\98.   9.48a.m.

143. If we will allow any part of our body to raise a complain for such burden it carry for us, then feet will be listed as Number one, as they carry us to where and to what step with no complain.

21\07\98.   9.55a.m.

144. If I have to win your love I must have it in real and not like a reflection on the mirror.

20/07/98   9.05p.m

145. Thank God the agonies within us are not to be seen, they are protected so we only feel the suffering within us.

21/07/99   10.00a.m

146. Disease and starvation is fatal war mankind has to fight; it is a war with no end till the day mankind will end.

2/07/98   9.34p.m

147. With a simple reason one can break a very good relation but it will be a very hard task to mend it again.

23/07/98   8.00p.m

148. He who expect too much gets disappointment very much.

                            25/07/9   8.45p.m

149. There are those who believe that success can be achieved through shortcut, many regrets for their trying as they end in a very wrong cut.

                            18/04/99   12.00p.m

150. You can treat life as you afford it and it has no saying, but can you afford if life treat you otherwise?

                            5\03\92.   10.17p.m.

151. Where can we find love, understanding and peace if we turn ourselves against each other?

                            12\12\91.   10.15p.m.

152. We should not point fingers at others shame when shame itself is within us.

                            28\03\92.   9.37a.m.

153. He who always remains silent when other speaks is not dumb, he can surprise others the day he will open his mouth.

                            22\01\92.   7,23p.m

154. Who will believe that there are some rich people who their dreams are envying poor people's life, but for many poor, their dreams wish are even for a day to be rich and enjoy life.

                            23\04\92.   7.58a.m

155. It is not bad attitude or shame to eat again a left over food as long as it will bring not harm but will save you from starving.

23\04\92. 8.20a.m

156. From you I am born, till this day I am known as a child from a wonderful mother, and I am proud of you. Today is a mother's day, may God bless you dear mother.

1991.

157. I did not know that injustice taste so bitter till that day I had experience it myself when truth did not won justice and only lie was regarded as truth.

24\04\92, 12.20p.m.

158. Sometime stubbornness can scare even a devil, he and can solve that problem of which no one dare to do.

29\04\92. 12.10a.m.

159. Consideration is necessary before one take wrong decision, though
It may delay the matter but should produce positive results.

160. Their are times when winning of the game is not very much important than winning the credit for the best performance of that game from all the fans.

8\05\92. 10.35a.m.

161. A person who hides his real identity because of his past history is a coward even to himself.

6\07\87.

162. It needs a very strong heart and courage for one to face the truth.

163. No force, no magic, not even history can return past back to the future.

164. One should be careful when reviling a secret; even walls do have ears sometimes.

28\05\92.   1.30p.m.

165. There are time and situation where one must hold his tongue and never to revile the truth, and if he lies just to protect the truth, then there is a risk and a price to pay.

28\05\92.   1.38p.m.

166. Some rich people are lack of talent, skill or manpower, some poor people are skilled, talented and hard working but lack of wealth, to survive and to allow the wheel of life turn for their sake, they must work together to meet their needs.

28\05\92.   4.00p.m.

167. To survive with what you have in your life is like to light many candle with one matchstick and not so many matchsticks to one candle.

11\09\92.   7.10p.m.

168. The value of a woman beauty is not to expose it to public but to preserve it and should be let to remain as mystery for anyone who seek to find out what lies behind that covered face.

8\10\92   12.05a.m.

169. A gift is a gift, no matter how cheap it is, it should be valued not for it cost but for that thought of whoever brought it to you.

11\11\92   10.52p.m

170. A good citizen is that who share his feelings to those who sacrifice their life to do to the best level their sense of duties for their people and country.

1\01\93.   10.43p.m.

171. He who witness unjust done to a weak person who could not defend himself because he is afraid of the strong, not that he portrayed himself as coward but he also betrayed his conscious as person of justice.

14\01\93.   5.25p.m.

172. No one should be forced to eat that forbidden fruit which is against his faith just for the sake of respecting other's culture and faith, what about his?

17\01\93.   4.50p.m.

173. One can be modern person, mingle with other's societies but never will he allow himself to loose his identity.

21\04\93   9.40p.m.

174. He who gave his word will never go against it, no matter what other say or do; he will stick to his word.

25\04\93   9/43p.m.

175. In the jungle even a predator becomes a prey, no matter how mighty he is.

18\05\93.   8.45p.m.

176. Supremacy does not mean that you force others to accept your terms and denying theirs.

17\05\93.   9.40p.m.

177. There are reasons that even rival should be friends, somewhere sometime somehow.

19\05\93.   9.04p.m.

178. For some good reasons, and sensibly we should agree that there are wrongs and rights and it is for us to judge which one is worth to be accepted.

18\05\93.   9.34p.m.

179. Why blaming the wind for your falling roof when the fact is, that your roof itself is not well fixed.

27\05\93.   8.50p.m.

180. What has happened today maybe it will not repeat again tomorrow, and what is there for us tomorrow, no one knows it today. Life is full of surprises.

27\05\93.   8.55p.m.

181. When stars in the sky starts to fade away and sound of birds and other living creatures is to be hard, then that is a sign of a new day to be born.

30\05\93.   6.23p.m.

182. Grieve and sadness is such pain and agony in our hearts that sometime just a beautiful smile from a loved one can be a best cure and relief.

11\06\93.   8.43p.m.

183. Make me to believe of what I do not believe, in facts, so I may have a faith to believe of what others believe.

7\01\94.   7.25p.m.

184. To a barber, a child's cry is not bothering him, but only to finish his job perfect, but it is a parent who brought that child to that barber who is tormented and feels pain of his child cry.

14\03\94.   7.30p.m.

185. I do not care or mind blame from other's just by doing the right thing, but I do mind if others oppose me for not allowing me to do the right thing.

14\03\94.   7.38p.m.

186. One can point out to other between wrong and right, time and time again and again, sometime one need luck to catch someone ears in listening to you.

14\05\94.   8.20p.m.

187. There is nothing wrong for a scholar in seeking more knowledge, as life has much to offer and one always has to learn. In this world nobody is perfect.

14\03\94.   8.33p.m.

188. Promise is a vow, it is a word of honour never to be broken, once given, and you can not go against it.

14\03\94.   8.40p.m.

189. When two strange people fell in love at first sight, they do not care much of so many obstacles of life are ahead in their life, till they come to realise that they belong to difference world.

14\03\94.   11.08p.m.

190. If your physical strength became weak and causes your life difficulties, then you should use strength of your mind to keep you strong so to enable you to face what so ever life comes ahead.

19\04\94.   11.45p.m.

191. If in life you have a secret enemy who brought so many miseries in your life, I think it is for your own good to find out who that enemy is, rather than to find out why he became your enemy, one can deal with that later.   19\04\94.   12.900p.m.

192. One will never know the meaning of peace of mind till he experiences difficulties.

4\05\94.   6.40p.m.

193. At last the runaway stream finds its way back to the river then why we fight for that water which belongs to all of us.

5\05\94.   11.35a.m.

194. One never knows his attitude well till others tell him.

15\05\94.   8.25a.m.

195. "I beg your pardon sir, Who are you to criticise my civilisation, culture and my heritage when you yourself did not qualify even with one among those."

21\05\94.   12.03a.m.

196. He who plants seed of evil will never eat its fruit.

6\06\96.   8.55p.m.

197. He who regards himself strong and mighty will get his match, and he who is weak never die alone.

12\06\96.   8.48p.m.

198. What feelings does a hunter hold in his heart when he hit a wrong victim and watching it running away to his death?

15\06\96.   1.25a.m.

199. It is very hard sometimes to image the outcome of our predictions,
A very sick person on the bed can survive and his visitor can die,
Of who dig a grave and who will be buried,
Of who choose a destination and who will reach there,
Of who propose for a neighbourhood mosque and who will have the privilege to pray in it? It is very hard for any one to predict what future store for us.

5\06\96.   9.50p.m.

200. A small penetration of light in a dark cave where one lost his way, gives hope for his life and surviving.

17\06\96.   10.05p.m.

201. Not every rusted thing is useless or to be thrown away, but tries to give them new life and another chance and you will be surprise of how strong they still are.

17\06\96.   9.45p.m.

202. Fate is not guided by stars; it is a happening which comes unaccepted to us by the will of God.

11\07\96.   1.00p.m.

203. Rain when it falls and pour and pour, some are happy while others regret and wish it did not.

11/07\96.   1.30p.m.

204. One should have the sense to understand and at least image the pain of the one who is hurt, maybe you will at least feel how he is suffering.

11\7\96.   1.38p.m.

205. If you want to be near to God, then try to avoid being close to Shaitan (Satan), the more you keep yourself away from him the more close you will be with God.

9\09\96.   1053p.m.

206. You can not ware shoes in your hands and a turban bind on your feet and expect people to accept it as normal, as each of these items have it right places to be wearer.

21/07096.   6.40p.m.

207. One should be ware when tighten a trousers belt, one wrong hole may hurt you or loose your trousers to drop down.

21\07\96.   6.45p m

208. Many men find that in a woman's heart their tenderness, kindness and even generosity but lack of the responsible to keep a secrets.

25\08\96.   8.15a.m.

209. There is no wound that does not pain, and there are cure which does not heal, no matter what medicine one uses.

9\09\96.   10.55p.m.

210. One only can defeat the suffering of the people who are oppressed not by their bodies strength but their faith and trust in uniting to deny the unjust done to them.

25\09\96.   1.44p.m.

211. Fruits are so attractive in their shape and colour, but the mystery of it that you eat of what you did not see and throw away of what has attracted you to buy.

5\10\96.   6.43p.m.

212. Judge me of my services which I render to you and not to what others tell you wrongly about me.

5\11\96.   7.55a.m.

213. When we grow old, we loose our body's strength and not are able to carry more burdens out of life, but we remain strong at heart even to carry the bitterness of life

22\11\96.   6.25p.m.

214. Does it matter which part of the ocean was rage and destroy my only boat? After all, the waves taste no difference; they are all cruel, salty and hard to swallow.

10\05\97.   5.55p.m.

215. In life there are many attitudes for one to experience, such as the bittersweet of the beginning or the sweet bitter of the ending on any fate, life has to offer.

27\097.   10.48p.m.

216. A house is a property and shelter one has to have, but a home is like a mothers womb where one always belong, one will never no a value of home till he own one.

24\05\97.   8.27p.m.

217. A sea traveller can change to travel in difference ships just to be comfort but he can not change the weather.

25\05\97.   9.56p.m.

218. Sometime things do change unaccepted, man best friend to turn into a foe or a worst enemy to be a very helpful person and become a great friend.

6\06\97.   11.40a.m.

219. There is no woman from the beginning of Adam & Eve knew what kind of a child she will bare from her womb, a king, a scholar a doctor, a killer or a thief, she only bare such a wonderful baby, shinning like a star in the sky, a very good looking being who when grow up may turn into one of the above character, Etc.,

8\06\97.   1.05p.m.

220. Is it necessary that we should prevail the truth every time, even though it will hurt us or that it may leave a scar in our heart? Can we not for the best sometime leave the truth alone, all alone to its hidden place, as we all know that not every truth is worth to listen to?

16\06\97.   8.00p.m.

221. Man have right to fulfil his ambition; to achieve them is his task.

17\06\97.   12.53.p.m.

222. If chilli and garlic are spices in our cooking, then laugh, surprises and jokes are also spices in our life.

19\06\97.   12.43p.m.

223. Justice is very costly to maintain, not financially or with a force power but with fairness, faithfulness and justice to it self

21\06\97.   12.38p.m.

224. In life, needs never end but in needs many lives end.

21\06\97.   10.10a.m.

225. We should be fair to accept, as fact should remain fact and not to be changed, if we write history it should be base on the fact, and those who read it should agree to accept the good, the bad and the ugly side of the fact.

22\06\97.   12.25p.m.

226. Money is necessary for our life needs, money is power, money is our energy but also is a source of corruption, money has the ability to change a strong into weak, a wise into a fool, honest to a cheater,

a faithful to a betrayer. There are those who became victims to give away their precious possession for it, and who will risk their lives in cheating death for it, but are there who are willing to care not for Mr. Money and survive without him?

22\06\97.   9.37p.m.

227. He, who falls in love with a rose, should bear in mind how protective roses are with their sharp thorns

25\06\97.   2.20p.m.

228. A messenger of love
A well wishers gift
A forgiveness seeker messenger
A queen of flowers
A wonderful God's creation by the name of Rose.

25\05\97.   2.55p.m.

229. Every artist has his own kind of recognition, and every art has its value.

20\6\97.   2.20p.m.

230. A human being has two journeys in his life, one that is welcome with celebrations and joy, while the other that ends with cries and mourns.

26\06\97.   8.25p.m.

231. One should not put blame to a whole nation for a sin of one wrong done by just one national

27\06\97.   8,35p.m.

232. He who has suffer and fall sick just by swallowing a sweet thing, can gain his health back also by swallowing the bitter pill.

1\07\97.   5.50p.m.

233. We care for the time, but does time care to wait for us?

1\07\97.   10.50p.m.

234. In business time means money, but in money business means nothing.

5\07\97.   12.24a.m.

235. Cruelty and kindness has nothing to do with faith, they are just our heart feelings, and occasionally even beasts do have the same feelings.

6\07\97.   5.55p.m.

236. Any fair question deserves honest answer

21\10\97.   1.31p.m.

237. If words will allow fact to speak for itself, then fact will never dare to bother words to speak

30\10\97.   1.45p.m.

238. The success of marriage is not counted on wealth or beauty of a person, but on trust, love and beloved truly ever after

3\11\97.   10.37p.m.

239. You can deny an invitation of a person to your wedding, but you can not deny him to invite you to his

4\11\97.   11.58p.m.

240. A creative artist sees his piece of work in his mind before others see it in reality.

5\11\97.   1.30p.m.

241. If you do not like something the way it is, try to change it for a better, but if you can not, then you better accept it the way it is and stay silence.

9\11\97.   10.18p.m.

242. So many steps to walk, so many destination to go, so many dreams to fulfil, yet fate and luck has its own roles to play.

8\07\97.   9,00p.m.

243. Love is not judged by a glimpse of a next person, it is a heavy subject which need consideration before one come to wrong conclusion.

13\07\97.   1.25p.m.

244. We should not judge the attitude of others for what they have done in the past, but of what they can offer for the future; why not let us give tomorrow a chance to bring for us the better and never the worst.

10\7\97.   8.29p.m.

245. Thoughts and facts are two difference things, our lives are facts, our thoughts are dreams, still dreams sometime can turn into fact, but never fact change in to a dream.

17\07\97.   9.13p.m.

246. Braves rarely cry, but when they have to, they do not shed tears in their eyes but cry within their hearts where their agony hides.

18\07\07.   6.24p.m.

247. Hope is like an energy we believe with it, weather things do happened or not, but hope is something we all need to live with.

19\07\97.   9.12p.m.

248. Success can never be achieved without struggle, determination and risk.

29\07\97.   10.30p.m.

249. There is time in our life where winnings will never be our guest, and then here is where we should be wise to accept losing as our guest.

16\10\97.   7.15P.M.

250. A mistake done, should not be the reason to allow misery and sorrows to overcome you all your life, but should be accepted sometime as a key which can open a door of no failure.

21\11\97.   7.30p.m.

251. Hating someone is an evil attitude and not a satisfaction within you, yet one gain nothing more of value than loosing others loves and friendship.

22\11\97.   9.48p.m.

252. The power of the government is from the people, but also the power of the people is from their government.

26\11\97.   11.00p.m.

253. If past has pasted and present is here, then from the present we should create a better future.

29\11\97.   7.42p.m.

254. One of my dreams to be fulfilling before I die is to turn my enemy into a friend and never allow my friend turn to be my enemy.

5\12\97.   9.05p.m.

255. It is not surprise in life to find you in grief today and happy tomorrow, as fate brings the unexpected in our life

3\12\97.   9.06p.m.

256. A brave can pretend to be weak with an act of weakness and people will be persuaded to believe him, but can a weak pretend to show braveness with an act which will make some people to believe him too.

12\12\97.   1.03p.m.

257. Beauty attracts many but only few can afford to have it.

11\12\97.   8.52p.m.

258. Why should we let doubts dominate our minds instead of giving consideration a priority to clear our doubts?

12\12\97.   11.30p.m.

259. A physical wound produce physical pain, spiritual wound has no physical pain but torment within.

16/12/94   12.34a.m

260. I can try to hide my face by not showing that I am crying because of the emotion of the suffering of others which has affected me, yet how can I hide and stop the shading of tears which by now they are half way flowing on my chicks, how can I hide them?

18/12/97   10.28p.m

261. Sometimes changes do cause problems for some and do better for others.

21/12/99   11.05p.m

262. If music can entertain my mind and not disturbing it or turn me in to a worst person rather than worth, than I will listen and enjoy to it and respect those who are behind its creation.

21/12/97   9.29p.m

263. When you image of peace, you should dream of it
When you speak of peace, you should respect it
When you fight for peace, you should be honest and value it
When you get that peace, you should safeguard it
With all your life.

25/12/97   9.25p.m

264. Trust is a very heavy and responsible burden for one to give other to safeguard it.

02/01/98   8.56p.m

265. Lies sound so wonderful and entertaining rather than truth, but sometimes end up into a very bore and loose faith to that person when truth brings fact openly.

02/01/98   9.31a.m

266. Understanding means to ease misunderstanding and not to cause it.

4\01\98.   9.55p.m.

267. Bad news bring disappointment or sorrows, and steal all the happy moods, but when bad news turn into good, they bring hope and happiness and even sometimes a little tears in the eyes, after all that is exactly what news are for.

4\01\98.   10.48p.m.

268. One should warn himself of a bad company he finds, as we all know that in our society no one accept bad as good and no good as bad.

7\01\98.   6.57p.m.

269. We being, have three places to live with, in a mother's womb, in this world and at the end in the grave.

7\01\98.   7.40p.m.

270. Love is a very sensitive seed, it need the right heart to grow.

8\01\98.   11.10a.m.

271. In life, though one will determine to do his best and avoid mistakes, but after all a human is a human, he is not fully completed, he may try all his best to turn all the stones turned and not one to leave unturned as he promise, but eyes may betray him and could pass one unnoticed.

8\01\98.   12.15p.m.

272. Any one who gives his opinion to others in their matter, should be willing to accept others decision too, wither they opposed or accepted, after all he only gives opinion and not decision.

8\101\98.   12.33p.m.

273. A crack in the wall that means a warning to repair it and live peaceful, ignores it and faces the consequences.

11\01\98.   12.55p.m.

274. When two people hurt each other's feelings, they should nurse each other wound and not only their personal wounds.

9\01\98.   1.00p.m.

275. A gentleman will never turn away his guest just because he disagrees with others guest's views.

12\01\98.   1.25p.m.

276. It is wonderful sometime for someone to bring back those good memories of the past just to entertain or remind others of what has happened.

12\01\98.   9.20p.m.

277. He who care not of nature's beauty, posse's ignorance heart.

13\01\98.   9.37p.m.

278. We can own wealth as well as other living creatures, but we belong to each other's as human being.

14\01\98.   1.10p.m.

279. One may not agree to one decision in the way he conducted his judgement, but yet that should not stop him to share his view for the goodwill of others.

15\01\98.   10.10p.m.

280. There is no bad of all bad or good and nothing but good only, in fact, where there are bad there must be one good seed hide beneath, only you need to pour water it will grow its way out to a fruitful tree which will benefit you all.

15\01\98.   10.18p.m.

281. Is it fare for that person who with hold his valuable opinion which can solve a major problem where others failed, just because those same others did not allowed him to give his opinion while he knows that his only opinion will save thousands from the disaster.

16\01\98.   9.05p.m.

282. Sometime a split-second decision can be the right judgement more than thoughts in saving a matter of emergency.

16\0198.   4.25.p.m.

283. Respect between two parents is must in front of their children; it is an attitude which should be inherited by their children

19\01\98.   1.00p.m.

284. I am willing to exchange one smiling moment just to be happy for the price of hundred sad hours if I have to.

20\01\98.   7.17p.m.

285. There is a very good reason behind that advice of "HEAR NO EVIL, SEE NO EVIL AND TALK NO EVIL" as where there is evil there is fear and sin.

23/01/98   10,23p.m.

286. It is not the age that counts when one is seeking an advice or an opinion from others but what most counts is the value of that advice.

23\01\98.   11.03p.m.

287. He, who has intentions, should have a very clear mind before he commits himself to them.

24\01098.   2.40p.m.

288. Truth is those words, which speaks for the fact, and not those, which penetrate into one ear and come out from another

24\01\98.   7.50p.m.

289. Knowledge is necessary for every one to have without discrimination, who knows one will do what for our mankind from that knowledge he has gain.

24\01\98.   11.13a.m.

290. Many of us sometime come to a wrong conclusion when judging a person by his appearance and not by what he is.

8\05\98.   10.40a.m.

291. The roots of tomorrow's problem are growing within us, only if we are willing to locate and destroy them, before tomorrow will still remain another dark day.

12\05\98.   9.40a.m.

292. To others, death is a scary thing and do not like the idea of it though it is a necessary end, to me, death is not a curse but a good omen for beautiful ending and wonderful begin which will never end.

16\05\98.   10.30p.m.

293. Beauty is unaccountable, not few but million of things, it only depends on one judgement, what you may find as ugly, it could the most beautiful by others.

20\05\98.   6.40p.m.

294. We must be cautious and bare in our minds that to preserve culture, tradition and heritage is a must under any price, if we will loose them we will pay very dearly for their return.

20\05\98.   8.00p.m.

295. Why should we teach our people to trust those who do not trust us before they teach their people to trust whom to trust them?

27\05\98.   1.38p.m.

296. When there are those who swimming in the sea, and one shout the word "SHARK", their will be panic, but in reality there are more dangerous creatures then shark in the sea, yet very few seems to bother.

12\06\98.   11.25a.m.

297. The test and delicious of a fruit is not judge by its look and colour of its skin but by taste.

30\05\98.   6.26a.m.

298. Do not let your healthy body mislead your mind to believe that no sickness can befall upon you; even a healthy and strong one can be a victim of any decease.

1\06\98.   5.45p.m.

299. Lies have many faces and many shapes, only truth remains the same.

1\06\98.   11.55p.m.

300. One to gain a true honest friend is worth than money, as money can never buy you a true friend.

5\06\98.   1.47p.m.

301. Good or bad time is not listed in our daily life program, but they are just around the corner, any time can knock our doors uninvited.

5\06\98.   11.55a.m.

302. We can build and destroy and rebuild again and again our homes, but what if we destroy our world, can we build it again?

11\06\98.   11.05a.m.

303. One can cross a low running river by throwing stones and boulders even if it take the whole day, what he needs is his ability and intention to do it.

11\10\98.   1.00p.m.

304. Ideas are sign of intelligent and creative mind, the best way to use one's idea for better results is to exchange them with other people's ideas, but one has to be careful not all people are fair.

12\06\98.   10.55a.m.

305. It is not your wealth that will make you look smart and know how to wear, many low earning people are very smart looking, what count most is a test of a person.

12\06\98.   11.28a.m.

306. Not all the smart brave can win against the weak.

12\06\98.   8.18p.m.

307. What is the use of wasting your energy to speak to those who pay not attention to what you are telling them?

13\06\98.   6.10p.m.

308. If you do not know, seek your answer of knowledge from those who have learned rather than those who never learned.

13\06\98.   10.30p.m.

309. Sometime destruction is necessary for the sake of construction.

15\06\98.   2.08a.m.

310. Any human life in danger is worth saving no matter whose.

16\06\98.   11.23p.m.

311. Every single living creature is entitled to live his natural way of life, then why are we trying to ignore the fact?

16\06\98.   11.23p.m.

312. It is a wrong belief to have, that only particular person is capable to do what he always doing and no other can.

17\06\98.   8.50p.m.

313. Jokes are entertaining our soul and mind and we happily laugh; yet too much jokes sometime may lead to unexpected results.

17\06\98.   8.55p.m.

314. There is quite a big faith difference between those who believe in Almighty God who is unseen and those who believe in idols and other images as their God.

17\06\98.   9.35p.m.

315. You can not maintain your physical youths all your living life, but mentally you can be young at heart all your life if you wish so.

18\06\98.   1.45a.m.

316. we buy land for our living purpose, but never bothers him to have a piece of land after our death, as we all know that piece of land is free.

20\06\98.   10.14a.m.

317. It is for better to take things which bother you out of your mind before it is too late to do so.

20\06\98.   10.30p.m.

318. If we can not change tomorrow to be a better day for us, then we should not have been the cause for that black yesterday which has brought misery and sorrow to our people.

20\06\98.   11.10p.m.

319. Why asking me to swallow the same thing which you yourself could not even put it near to your mouth.

21\06\98.   6.01a.m.

320. Competition is a challenge one has to stick with it to the end, as they say, quitter never wins and a challenger never quit.

21\06\98.   6.15a.m.

321. Photographs are reminders of the past and history for the future.

17\05\97.

322. Let us not point accusation fingers at each other, and spoil the good relation between us just for merely doubts of no solid ground proof, let fact speak for itself

21\06\98.   9.40p.m.

323. Take what life can give you and give what you can afford and make it as principle for a better life ahead of you.

23\06\98.   6.43a.m.

324. Even once in a lifetime, someone should try to be somebody out of nobody.

3\07\98.   9.33p.m.

325. He, who knows somebody wells, can recognise him even from his back out of many people.

3\07\98.   9.37p.m.

326. People are created equal in many ways, the only difference is their sense of mind, which create different ideas.

5\07\98.   8.52p.m.

327. If we will not insist ourselves to form the habit of respecting one another's faith, then our future generations will never have

understanding trust and respect to each other faith, we will be a nation with separate path to follow.

6\07\98. 1.10a.m.

328. Not all comedians make people laugh; some are just waste of time.

8\07\98. 10.35p.m.

329. A beauty of an old person still remain with her by a judgement of another person of her same age, to him, she was beautiful, she is now and will remain forever beauty.

9\07\98. 6.20p.m.

330. A person who has patience live better life than that who doesn't.

9\07\98. 6.40p.m.

331. Why we let ourselves rule our lives as bosses in the office, why can't we live as husband and wife and find the real meaning of happiness life to enjoy.

9\07\98. 6.57p.m.

332. A remarried of divorced couple is like mending a broken verse where cracks still exist.

9\07\98. 11.14p.m.

333. If we care to build a bright future for our nation, then we must try to reduce burden of responsibility by helping our people to help their government in implementing their needs for their bright future years to come.

12\07\98. 10.47a.m.

334. In any international games tournaments, the end brings joy and happiness for celebration for winners, and disappointments to losers, but that is exactly what games are for, but most important, is to have that privilege of participation in such big event, It is an honour.

13\07\98.   12.17a.m.

335. It should not be a jealousy or a cunning that should be a reason to be a better person than your rival, but have the spirit of invyness and prove that you also can be better.

13\07\98.   8.52p.m.

336. Not until we face with difficulties and obstacles, then we should care for our lives careful. Why not now?

16\07\98.   8.10a.m.

337. He who respect his superior with humbleness of "YES SIR" does not mean that is sign of weakness, but respect and to honour others morality, and in return one is regarded as a noble and a gentleman. Obeying is not slavery.

20\04\98.   7.48p.m.

338. If there are any obstacles between two loving people, together they should remove them with understanding and bid them good-bye.

30\01\98.   11.30p.m.

339. If we do not value our past then the future will not have any credit.

1\02\98.   8.00p.m.

340. It is a duty of any doctor to save life even of a wounded enemy or a wounded suspected criminal and never ignore him for his crime, but give him his life back and a chance to prove his innocence.

19\02\98.   12.45a.m.

341. A good quality of a person lies not in his position he held but in his heart and how he treats others.

22\02\98.   8.10p.m.

342. People happiness lies within their hearts and souls, when they are sad and sorrow, it shows on their faces.

22\02\98.   8.20p.m.

343. I can not accept to believe that I will be here to meet tomorrow but I face it, but within me there is a hope that tomorrow will come.

8\03\98.   9.17p.m.

344. Propaganda are lies just to pursued other to have in you, mostly it is used by politicians to gain supremacy of what their targets are and never for the good will of their people but mostly of their own.

8\03\98.   9.15p.m.

345. Truth is truth, but can never remain truth until people believe in it as truth.

9\03\98.   1.13a.m.

346. How shock I was when I came to find out that in that sweet speaking mouth there is venom hidden its tongue, ready to kill.

16\04\98.   9.38p.m.

347. Changing of appearance will never make someone to change his attitudes.

17\10\98.   9.37p.m.

348. They say beauty lies in the eyes of the beholder; I say not only the eyes, but the heart and the mind of a beholder.

17\10\98.   8.07p.m.

349. I would rather remain penniless but trusted and faithful rather then a corrupter and cunning with bad reputation for earning my living.

19\10\98.   8.35p.m.

350. To safeguard the king, one does not build a fort in the palace but the palace in a fort.

20\10\98.   11.10p.m.

351. There are living creatures living within us that can eat and destroy even the iron wall built to safeguard ourselves, these creatures are within us, among us and look same like us.

210\98.   11.15p.m.

352. We sometimes should accept nature as it is, rather then trying to change it for a better look.

5\11\98.   8.55p.m.

353. Wild life environment is worth protected, but if we can not protect ourselves from it then who will protect it from us.

5\11\98.   10.55p.m.

354. Lie is sin as well as forbidden both by God and in our society, but defending a liar is more worst sin, as it is an evil act beyond doubt.

6\12\98.   3.18a.m.

355. Sometime fools live better life than wises, as they care no much as what wise people know.

19\11\98.   8.55p.m.

356. When lies become strong to survive then truth will have no place to live.

19\11.98.   11.00p.m.

357. Ask me, why I am so concern of the past I knew and grew with? My answer is, because, I would like our children and the future generation to come to know it, be proud of it and by all means preserve it.

15\11\98.   12.05a.m.

358. When I came in this world, I became a burden to my parents but I gained their love, I grew to live and learn till this day where I had my first child and know that he too will be my burden to carry and be a wonderful human to love his children.

16\10\98.   9.55p.m.

359. Yesterday is history, today is news, tomorrow is unpredicted dream, who will be there to meet it and who will miss it that remains a mystery.

5\10\98.   10.05p.m.

360. Behind every successful student there is a very good teacher.

10\10\94.   8.33p.m.

361. Knife is an instrument meant to cut things with, it works both ways, by pushing forward or pulling back, but if an accident occur, knife is not to be blamed.

8\10\94.

362. I am not a miracle maker, do not expect impossible from me. I can not build a strong fort to protect you with just old broken tools.

10\10\94.   9.05p.m.

363. He, who holds a diamond carelessly with his fingers, should blame himself when it falls and break or lost.

2\11\94.   6.15p.m.

364. A wise person is he who admits a fault is a fault, and should be avoided not to repeat again, SORRY is not an excuse enough to correct it.

3\11\94.   11.30p.m.

365. A person has to sacrifice so many things of his life for the sake of his family. To him it is a principal way of responsibility.

27\11\94.   10.10a.m.

366. He who his feelings were hutted by someone, can forgive but never forget.

30\11\94.   10.55p.m.

367. Life is a challenge, one has to accept that challenges either to win or to lose, herewith then one will know the exactly meaning of life.

2\12\94.   4.55p.m.

368. He, who always wins, will never understand the meaning of defeat until he experience it.

2\12\94.   2.28p.m.

369. A person who made history someday he will die, but what he has left behind of his history, will always remain.

7\12\94.   10.00p.m.

370. Trust no one when trust is no longer available between you.

3\01\95.   6.20a.m.

371. Do not be surprised if I tell you that I witness a beast act more humanly than human and a human being became so beastly then beast.

28\194.   9.26.p.m.

372. He who care for education, and respect to receive the wisdom of knowledge will struggle to learn from his teachers till he acquire their knowledge, yet he should teach others who also seeks education and knowledge so they too can gain that light of life.

4\01\95.   8.25p.m.

373. "A very good morning to you sir, I am sorry I can not give you my hand for shaking" said a young mechanic man to an old passer-by, the old man replied, "Son! Those dirty hands of yours are

blessing hands, one should be proud to touch them, please allow me to have the honour of shaking them" and the young with a big smile on his face took the hand of his old friend man and shake it.

6\01\95.   7.35p.m.

374. Sometime no words can possible express exactly the inner feelings of a person. Some of unexplained feelings can not be understood, neither by words or expression.

25\08\95.   12.20a.m.

375. Even some poor of the poorest can have life full of happiness and joy rather then those richer of the riches.

19\09\95.   10.30p.m.

376. Peace, every single soul in this world wishes to have it, spoken of it in thousands of languages, can be found in dictionaries, understood well it's meaning and it's aim clearly, yet, there are those who ignores its morality and fundamental aim. Majority speaks about it, few respect it, but many die and suffer for it.

21\09\95.   1.15.p.m.

377. If we believe that peace is a necessary commitment to all mankind's, then let us not deny it to others.

28\9\95.   9.30p.m.

378. He, who shut his mouth and hide your secret, can open it any time you reveal his secret.

15\10\95.   8.05p.m.

379. Until we travel to our destination, no matter how hardship one can experience with rough roads and a far away distance, so what! We should not turn back, but proceed to the end. This is where you will find the real meaning of achieving your target.

16\10\95.   7.35p.m.

380. Trust is risk and responsible to give to anybody, and so it is difficult to find the right person to trust, but how one can judge a trust person?

19\10\95.   8.15a.m.

381 We should make the most of our time useful and do something worth that we will remember all our lifetime. The gone time will never come back again.

20\10\95.   6.50p.m.

382 Day dreaming is just an imaginative hope to entertain one's mind and heart, there is no reality in it.

24\10\95.   8.50p.m.

383. To live with hope for a better tomorrow is worth, as there are many tomorrows to come, any one of them may ring your bell of hope.

24\10\95.   10.51p.m.

384. Hate-rade is a worst disease one to have within his heart, if you will not cure it sooner, then it will spread from one soul to the others.

6\11\95.   10.40p.m.

385. He who decide to go ahead with his good plan should do so without looking back, otherwise he might come to see of what he did not expect ct to see which can make him to change his mind.

12\11\95.   7.30p.m.

386. Calling a person "PIG" is an insulting, it may hurts his feelings and would mind it, and may be even be a reason to start a quarrel, but for a change try to call any pig "HUMAN", will he care?

12\11\95.   7.55p.m.

387. There are two roads we always pass through in life, a road from mother's womb to this world, and a road from this world to the earth womb.

22\11\95.   7.00p.m.

388. In life, one should make his wealth as a slave to serve him and never allow the wealth to be his master.

22\11\95.   7.10p

389. Even the best and well skilled craft man can not produce the best of his work without the right tools.

4\12\95.   10.30p.m.

390. A good wise teacher does not only just teach his students, but also learn from them of so many things he did not experience before; here is where he will find a success in believing that from student's teachers also can learn.

8\12\95.   12.07a.m.

391. We often never point our guns to shoot and kill that person who killed a wild life animal, but we will hunt and destroy that animal which tried to kill any human being.

10\12\95.   12.03a.m.

392. Why should I bother to join that club of surviving when death is a necessary end and no one can avoid it?

9\12\95.   11.40p.m.

393. There is a time when death has less pain than torments in the heart.

10\12\95.   10.42p.m.

394. It is very slow moving and kill my patience, yet it will arrive thou late and for sure it will leave us and only it's memory will remain, that is what time is and for

13\12\95.   8.50a.m.

395. A day before the last day was far better than that night before the beginning of the tension, which was caused by those who never care for our mankind to survive.

22\12\95.   10.50p.m.

396. You can accuse a person as your enemy, but do not expect others to do the same on him, as an enemy to you can be a friend to others.

10\3\96.   11.45p.m.

397. All of what happened yesterday can not happen again the same tomorrow.

3\04\96.   1.10a.m.

398. The beauty of a fruit is what you eat of it and not of what has tempted you to buy it.

6\04\96.   11.45p.m.

399. What is the use of a mousetrap, which has caught our cat, the intruder is still running around, as our mouse catcher is no longer existing, died in that trap.

9\04\96.   9.45p.m.

400. One does not throw away a plate because of its cup is broken.

9\04\96.   8.40p.m.

401. Home is the only place that one feel secure and find happiness as well as a peace of mind, that is why they called it "HOME SWEET HOME".

9\04\96.   8.50p.m.

402. Hand by hand, pain by pain and stone by stone, the people has built the wall with tears, that wall with fear, where so many died and buried there, and today that wall is among the seven wonders of the world and their children are so proud for what their parents have scarified and left for them and for all the people of the world to witness that great wall of China.

10\04\96.   12.23a.m.

403. Even kings do envy that normal life which many of his subjects are enjoying with, sometime he wish he can forget that he is a king and experience that freedom every one has.

13\04\96.   10.20p.m.

404. Sometime co-operation is a key to a success.

6\05\96.   12.13p.m

405A friend will never hurt his friend feelings; he who did that does not know the value of friendship.

204\96.   11.40p.m.

406. Beauty is where what eyes can see and what heart can accept.

9\05\96.   8.06p.m.

407. A secret is safe only in that strong heart and never in a weak and a torn one, as there is no safer place to safeguard the secret then a heart.

16\7\96.   12.35p.m.

408. In a race, it is simple to be on the starting line, but very hard to compete and to reach a finish line.

29\11\98.   9.30p.m.

409. No one can judge himself as a better or worth person until told by others.

26\11\98.   10.10p.m.

410. One should not be worry when others talked loudly about him but when they whisper.

29\11\98.   9.10p.m.

411. Moral respect is the right cloths for one to wear, and shame is the last drink to drink in one's life as that drink will never quench his thirsty for respect.

13\12\98.   10.39p.m.

412. One can put the exact amount of sugar in his cup of tea, but will never get the exact taste if he will not stir the tea.

8\12\98.   12.03p.m.

413. For some reasons, sometime it is worth to be helpful and sometime one regret he did it.

9\12\98.   9.00p.m.

414. Money is the main source of getting you of what you want, knowledge is the main source of making you of what you want to be.

11\12\98.   11.27p.m.

415. Any good teacher feels proud of his student's success, but also the students should be thankful and proud for such pain their teachers took for them till they have learned, understood and achieve their success.

11\12\98.   11.44p.m.

416. It is not fare to put the blame on all the people for the crime committed by one person.

14\12\98.   12.10a.m.

417. Not in any books of God, mentioned that earth belongs only to us human beings and not to other creatures as well.

12\12\98.   9.00p.m.

418. Home is a place one feels proud to be no matter how small or untidy it is.

14\12\98.   11.52p.m.

419. He who wants to climb the mountain, needs the strength, determination and a healthy body, to reach to the top he needs luck.

15\12\98.   5.25p.m

420. There is no peace, which can be obtained without paying price and sacrifices.

15\12\98.   7.25p.m.

421. Why should one try to run away because he can not face the truth, rather he should stand-by to welcome it face to face and never run.

15\12\98.   7.35p.m.

422. An artist should have all the freedom of expression to enable him to follow his vision of what his creating.

15\12\98.   7.40p.m.

423. Should one believe in his new friend who was his enemy before, or his new rival who was also his friend before?

15\12\98.   9.23p.m.

424. If yesterday was not a bright day for us, then that is not the end of the world, tomorrow can be brighter with hope.

15\12\98.   9.30p.m.

425. One should not refuse the helping hand from a good samatarian just because he belongs to an opposite cult.

18\12\98.   11.40a.m.

426. If winning is a pride then losing is not a shame, but a hard luck.

18\12\98.   6.03p.m.

427. Winning of war does not depend on the best of the weapons or majority of fighting soldiers, but the masterminds who are leading that war.

18\12\98.   6.12p.m.

428. For the sake of my country and my people, it is wise and worth for me to die for them, rather then allowing them to shed their blood and sacrifice the whole nation to die for me.

18\12\98.   6.15p.m.

429. I made my mistakes yesterday; I do not want to do it again today, as I do not know what day tomorrow will be.

18\12\98.   6.25p.m.

430. What is the use of your visit to my grave and always cry? Why did you not pray for my soul since that day I died?

21\12\98.   11.30p.m.

431. Any heart, which does not have faith, does not have love.

23\12\98.   1.00a.m.

432. Saying of wisdom means to say in short but mean a lot.

22\12\98.   11.00a.m.

433. Not all surprises are for better, there are also not good surprises that are why others do not like surprises.

2\01\99.   2.20a.m.

434. In anger sometime we do say of what we do not mean, but when we are normal, do we always mean of what we have said.

2\01\99.   2.28a.m.

435. One will never know the value of missing until he experiences it.

3\01\99.   4.10p.m.

436. We may be born from the same stomach, but differ in many things in our lives, this is natural and normal.

3\01\99.   9.07p.m.

437. Do we realise that we do affect our children minds if we urge or quarrel in front of them? Ask them if you dare, and be preparing for the surprise answers.

3\01\99.   9.21p.m.

438. When a child has been involving himself into some problem, it is the parents who suffer most, for that love they hold for their children.

3\01\99.   10.45p.m.

439. If you care, then give to that person who is in need, even if he did not ask for your help.

3\01\99.   10.55p.m.

440. Those that are planning to turn our world into a hell of a place for us to live, and then they should also plan not to bare any more children, as there will be no safer place for those children to live.

4\01\99.   1.30p.m.

441. It is wrong to hate someone without any reason of your own, just because someone else did not like him.

9\01\99.   9.17p.m.

442. Some happenings which come by fluke ends up with good surprise.

1\01\99.   10.10p.m.

453. A person appearance will never show his evils which hidden within him.

12\01\99.   11.25p.m.

444. No wise person will be willing to destroy his reputation for the sake of helping the wrong doers.

16\01\99.   3.06p.m.

445. We should teach ourselves to accept that person who's knowledge can help us to solve our major life problem and will help our country to achieve that goal where many failed, no matter where he come from, without discriminating him.

16\01\99.   7.07p.m.

446. He, who can blow the trumpet, will make others to dance.

9\01\99.   12.06a.m.

447. One who fear another person, should not fear him physical but of what hidden in his mind and in his heart.

19\01\99.   12.20a.m.

448. I need to trust my wealth to someone as care taker, should I trust a rich who fears poorness or a poor who dreams for richness?

19\01\99.   11.03p.m.

459. If insult and swearing does hurt your feelings then do not use it to others.

20\01\99.   9.55p.m.

450. There was a time when we did not care about our wrongdoing, but now come the time where we regret of that and wished we didn't.

20\01\99.   12.03a.m.

451. We should not put blame on God for our errors done and all because we do not like to be blamed.

20\01\99.   11.03p.m.

452. It needs courage and wisdom to train a lion to eat in your hand without harming you.

21\01\99.   1.50p.m.

453. I am willing to be called an idiot and stupid but earn a heaven rather then called smart and brave and earn hell.

21\01\99.   1.55p.m.

454. He who achieve business profits and enjoy the sweet life, find it very difficult to face the loss and a beginning of a bitter life.

20\01\99.   11.32p.m.

455. Every generation left behind a history for the coming generation to know and learn of what has happened in their past.

23\01\99.   11.30p.m.

456. There is willpower in every one of us, only it needs one to awaken it, even a coward can turn into a brave person.

23\01\99.   5.37p.m.

457. If you ask me which among all the wealth on earth is offering to me to, among all I will choose only three, AIR, WATER and FOOD, remaining worth nothing to me.

23\01\99.   8.45p.m.

458. Anger sometime brings more harms than cure if one does not cool his heart and use wisdom.

24\01\99.   1.40p.m.

459. It is not the wealth which can bring up a child to be a better person, there are so many things where money is not necessary, but can be obtained from our parents.

26\01\99.   9.35p.m.

460. A breach of promise by a person makes him worth nothing, even for one cent is not worth to value him.

28\01\99.   9.33p.m.

461. It is sin to expose lies to something happened and it is more sinners to create lies on something never happened

31\01\99.   4.55p.m.

462. There is nothing wrong to tell our children of others people wrong done so as not for them to do the same.

6\02\99.   11.53p.m.

463. Where there is a dream there is hope
Where there is a way there is a will
Where there is a risk there must be courage.

7\02\99.   12.20a.m.

464. What good is there for one to accept an end when he was denied of the beginning?

7\02\99.   12.45a.m.

465. He, who is met with sad moments, should try to bring back past memories just to entertain his mind and allow sorrow and sadness to dissolve away.

7\02\99.   7.47p.m.

466. Curiosity is a habit sometime it is worth having it, it is a human nature to find about things and facts.

11\02\99.   9.00p.m.

467. It is easy to destroy a bridge but a very hard task to rebuild it again and what the price one has to pay for its construction.

11\02\99.   11.50p.m.

468. There are some among us who believe in what other said, but there are those who believe in facts and sincere judgement, they work very hard till they get it.

13\02\99.   4.44p.m.

469. A man can say he is a man enough to that task and need people to believe him, but to others he has to prove his words.

1

470. So many happenings in our life teach us so many things, which taught us to create a better life.

19\02\99.   12.00a.m

471. Seeking wisdom from the elders, one has to travel very far away with so many obstacles and hardship in his route but it is worth to have them.

20\2\99.   10.50a.m.

472. We human like to eat but hate to spit.

21\02\99.   12.00p.m.

473. Revenge brings no more then miseries within us until we grew that tree of love, which can bare a very sweet fruits of good relation

21\02\99.   2.20p.m.

474. He, who is alone and has no one in his life, should be given a chance to live with others and feel that he also belong in the society. \

21\02\99.   8.03p.m.

475. When will our children learn to look straight in our faces and say without shame "YES, I DID IT" instead of telling lies just to protect their skins?

20\02\99.   11.03p.m.

476. He who holds a stoned heart will never understand the meaning of the human feelings.

22\02\99.   11.15p.m.

477. Talent is not a gift, but tough learning days to achieve it.

3\03\99.   1.38p.m.

478. You can not believe a person again once he lied to you, but for some necessary reason or another you can try to trust him.

4\03\99.   23.30p.m.

479. Once did a mistake will always remain as a mistake and should be avoided not to be repeated again.

5\03\99.   9.50p.m.

480. So much laughing sometime ends with tears,

6\03\99.   11.40a.m.

481. Standard must be obtained for selling our products; otherwise we will destroy our reputation and the name of our country.

14\03\99.   8.40p.m.

482. If I have to choose between two, I would prefer to be a human rather then a person.

15\03\99.   11.31p.m.

483. Every bright morning has a dark night but not every dark night has a bright morning.

16\03\99.   9.55p.m.

484. Love has no time limit, never say too late to fall in love.

17\03\99.   7.17p.m.

485. One should not spread the past wrong done by others as sins, it could be that God has already forgiven them while you are committing one of the unforgiving sin

27\03\99.   8.43p.m.

486. He who does not accept criticism is not fare in his judgement and he who ignored fact has also ignored justice.

22\03\99.   10.55p.m.

487. When we point our fingers to those who ignore democracy then we should make sure that we are the first to implement it.

28\03\99.   7/10p.m.

488. You need to understand the value of education; here then you will be among those who fight against literacy.

30\03\99.   12.17a.m.

489. He who did not take care of his children's necessary needs because of his ignorance, then it will come the day those same children will ask him why.

7\05\99.   9.13p.m.

490. They ignore the danger and try to cheat death just to gain prestige and popularity by winning the game, none of them realise the value of life until someone does something wrong.

7\05\99.   9.30p.m.

491. If every country in this world will preserve its heritage and culture and not copying others, then for sure there will be much to learn and exchange between nations.

8\05\99.   5.38p.m.

492. He who feels shame of his past is a coward to face the future.

8/05/99   6.20a.m.

493. Feeling guilty is normal to many who did wrong though no one know about him, yet his memories will never leave him to forget.

8\05\99.   11.20p.m.

494. Sometime one have to be brave and strong just to overcome the weakness buried within him as to face what life can bring ahead of him.

9\05\99.   12.03a.m.

495. How I wished someone can give me a portion of his love just to dissolve the pain of agony in my heart.

9\05\99.   12.15a.m.

496. If imaginations are fantasies and people are enjoying to ride on them, then I have plenty to offer.

9\05\99.   12.40a.m.

497. There was time I wished if I would be able to see within my heart and find out how strong and faithful my heart is.

9\05\99.   1.02a.m.

498. What so ever which did not come the way one expected today, and his entire dream went wrong, then that is not the last day of the world, tomorrow can be the right day, one must leave with hope.

9\05\99.   1.18a.m.

499. One does not spit on the same plate he eats with, and he who does is more animal than human.

9\05\99.   10.10p.m.

500. If heart does have ears, then for sure my heart heard your heart's whispering those words of true love you have always treasure for me.

10\5\99.   12.16a.m.

501. Never say "YES" when you feel shy to say "NO", and never say "NO" and regret it afterwards. Use always the right word on the right moment.

11\05\99.   12.30a.m.

502. In life, one can gain many friends, but he also can have enemies unknown to him.

11\05\99.   10.17p.m.

503. From experience, one can learn and teach others too.

12\05\99.   12.12a.m.

504. IF you are satisfied of what you got today, then you should work harder to make tomorrow more better then today.

14\05\99.   12.25a.m.

505. My friend asked for my advice on how to save the time in his planning journey, I told him "Stop asking more questions and start your journey now, you will save much time".

20\05\99.   6.34p.m.

506. If one have for some reason a heat of misunderstanding, then he should cool his heart to deal with the matters.

20\05\99.   10.45p.m.

507. When a night ends, a bright morning appears even if the sun did not come out, we call it that another day and never a long night yesterday.

21\05\99.   9.23p.m.

508. Living in one area will never make you know your country better, try to move around and visit other places, you will be surprise what treasure of beauty your country posses.

23\05\99.   12.45p.m.

509. A brave person is that who accept the challenge of life and not that with body full of muscles.

23\05\99.   8.12a.m.

510. He who does not like to lend his ears to others when they speak, should also close his mouth and say nothing to them.

23\05\99.   10.32p.m.

511. To beat a champion is not to end his championship once and for all; he may rise and win again and again.

23\05\99.   11.37p.m.

512. A strong phrase of philosophy words, can change someone's mind decision in a split of a second and do the otherwise.

20/9/2012-   2140hrs.

You can not wash away blood with blood but with any liquidity.

4-10-2012. -   1315hrs.

You can not stop the two nations war with another war but with sensible and wisdom dialogue and never to side on any nation but with equal judgment.

4-10-2012 -   1320hrs.

He who does not mind his language when talking to others, ends up in many to ignore him and lost fri I can bear to face an anger of a person face to face whom I know before, but I do not have the heart to face fear of a person I do not know or see before.

20th January   2055 hrs.

2. Past no matter how bitter and hard it was, should not be ignore or forgotten but should be like a page to learn with and teach others of how to build a better future.

A person who always consider a matter before he make his judgement should be known as wise philosopher,

4th March 2013. –   2245hrs,

If you are not in your habit to thank God for what it has create for you and others, then my brother at list thank him for creating a tree which gives you shade when you are in a sun, it gives you fruits when you hungry, it produce flowers to decorate the place when there is no colors around, it gives you timber to make things to live with, yet if you are not thankful to God my brother, then you should learn to be thankful, as you are also part of God creation.

18-7-2014 – 1.30am

Do not hate yourself because you did not have 3 important things in life, good looking, fortune and talent, pretend to believe that they are not important more than you, as in reality a person is more important than many things in the whole world. Things have no value without a person. 24th June 2014 – 2150hrs.

Do not underestimate the value of a Baisa, as it is a baisa which can make a Rial, and a rial is an energy, that energy which give support to a life, that life which we all fighting to maintain it, preserve it, enjoy with it safely and happily ever after but only on this planet earth and no money will maintain its value after we leave this world. 23rd June 2014 – 05.00 am

And that with all their help today I have been able to finish this book of collection of more than 500 thoughts created by me for my reader to read, learn and teach or use these phrases of wisdom as good knowledge to others for the better purpose of our daily life.

Many thanks also goes to all who gave their supports as sponsors and those who shared their most valuable time in correcting, advising and support my ambition of publishing this book of mine for many to read.

Jawad Ibrahim Ahmed Al Bahrani.